No More Battles

with
Strong-Willed
Kids

Maryln Appelbaum

Published by Appelbaum Training Institute
104 Industrial Boulevard, Suite A
Sugar Land, TX 77478
1 800-23-CHILD
www.atiseminars.org

h. Jokinen

Printed in the United States of America
ISBN 0-9777189-7-2

Appelbaum Training Institute
Houston, Texas

It takes two for there to be a power struggle.

Table of Contents

Introduction

There are some children who always want to have their own way. They push and pull and do everything in their power to have things be the way they want it to be. They are usually known as strong-willed children! As infants they may scream and yell when they are not held constantly. Some children seem to control their parents from the very beginning. The parents are not in charge of the home, the children are.

Once they get their way, they are only satisfied for a short period of time, until there is something else that they want, and the struggle begins anew. The more they get what they want, the more they want. It becomes a vicious cycle. They have a unique ability to hold out for what they want. They are persistent.

Actually, these children can grow into powerful leaders. They have leadership ability in how they manage to control the world around them. Yet, unless something is done early on, they will not be kind and benevolent leaders; they will be dictators who simply want what they want when they want it. This book will give you strategies to help these children grow into their leadership roles--to be wise and caring leaders.

Chapter 1
How Do Children Become Strong-Willed?

There are two reasons children become strong-willed. One reason is they are simply born that way. They are born fiercely independent. Parents report that these children are different from their other children. The children want what they want when they want it. They cry and cry to get what they want. Of course, eventually the parent gives in. As soon as the parent gives in, the child learns, "Aha, I can get what I want when I want it. I just have to hold out long enough."

The second reason is that children are systematically but unintentionally trained to be strong-willed. This training occurs when families automatically give in to children providing them with whatever they want whenever they want it. They let children rule the roost. They may do this out of love. Here is a scenario. Little "Payton" is the first-born son of the Jamison's. They waited a long time to have a baby. When Payton was finally born, they were thrilled. They had a beautiful nursery set up for him. Right from the beginning, they hated to hear him cry. They carried him in their laps. They snuggled him constantly. Whenever he cried for anything or even reached out for something, they made sure he got it. After awhile Payton learned that he could get anything he wanted from his parents. If he wanted to be held, he simply had to cry. If he wanted a new toy, he simply had to point. The world was his oyster! He was getting heavier and heavier to carry around. Mrs. Jamison decided he should have his own little chair for meals rather than sit in their laps. The first time she put him there, it felt strange to him so he cried. Mrs. Jamison could not stand hearing him cry, so she picked him up again. Another time,

Mrs. Jamison's sister and brother-in-law came over with their little boy, Timmy, who was the same age as Payton. Timmy was playing with a toy he brought from home. Payton wanted the toy and cried and shrieked to get the toy. Mrs. Jamison finally asked her nephew, Timmy, to give his toy to Payton. She just couldn't stand to hear him cry. The power struggles had begun and with each new day, Payton was learning that he could emerge victorious. Mr. and Mrs. Jamison reached the point where even though they loved their child, they found it difficult to handle him. It was hard for them to always meet his demands. They could not get him to go to sleep at night. They couldn't get him to eat his meals when it was meal time. Everything was a struggle. They tried to go out and have an evening alone, but the babysitter simply couldn't handle Payton and refused to baby-sit for him. They enrolled him in a child care preschool program, but the preschool program also was struggling with Payton. Everything was a struggle. When he didn't get what he wanted, he yelled and yelled until someone always gave in just to stop the noise. He had been unintentionally trained to get whatever he wanted whenever he wanted it.

Children like Payton need help. They need to learn how to interact with others. They need to learn how to be more sensitive to the needs of others. They need to learn how to be kind. They need to learn how to say "yes" instead of "no" all the time. This book will teach you the skills you need to help these children like Payton. The "Payton's" of the world need your help.

Here is another story – this time of a young and beautiful woman who had grown up in a similar fashion to Payton. Megan had been a pretty child with big brown eyes and a wonderful smile that lit up her whole face when she was happy. Megan grew accustomed to getting what she wanted at home. Social life at school was a struggle for her. She was bright academically, but she wanted things her own way. She had a hard time making and keeping friends because of this. She had a few friends who let her be the leader, but they would soon tire of this. When she became sixteen, she got her driver's license, and her parents bought her a beautiful new car. When she graduated from high school, they got her another new car. They gave her a credit card so she could buy all the clothes she wanted. She went on to college but struggled because she was just one of many students there. She could not get her bearings. She decided to become an airline stewardess. At the age of twenty-two, her parents decided to cut off her credit cards and let her function on her own. She was totally frustrated. When she heard about this book being written to help others, she said: "I can't hold a relationship with any guy. They find me too demanding. This is the first job I have had to have. I don't know how to manage money. I have always had everything given to me. I have few close friends." She said, "Tell others not to do that to their children." This beautiful young woman was lonely and struggling now to grow up, to become independent. The very thing her parents wanted for her—for her to become independent, didn't work. She was in fact truly dependent. She was dependent on others to meet her needs and did not know how to manage in the big world on her own.

This is a very important concept. When children are given everything they ask for, they are in actuality, not learning to be independent and self-sufficient. They are learning instead to be dependent! They are dependent on others to meet their needs. They only have learned how to ask for what they want and to manipulate. They have not actually learned how to be self-sufficient. You need to help your children so this does not happen to them.

Your goal is to prepare children for life in a more positive way. Life is full of ups and downs, bumps and grinds. Children need to learn how to manage their lives to get through the bumps and grinds. They need to learn how to set goals and follow through. The goal has to be more than just getting an adult in their life to do it for them. They will never become independent that way. They need to learn how to be independent, kind, and caring people.

Chapter 2
Preventing Power Struggles

Freedom within Limits—Take Charge!

Caregivers and parents need to take charge. This is very important. Children need boundaries and limits. When they are allowed to do anything they want when-ever they want to do it, it doesn't promote independence. It instead promotes acting out. They are not ready for unlimited freedom. They need freedom within limits. Have you ever gone to a huge sale in a department store? The store doors open at 7 a.m. The parking lot is filled with cars and people. The lines waiting to get in are enormous. People are feeling anxious to get what they want –to be first to find some great bargain. Once the doors are opened, there is a huge rush to different aisles where everything is marked down for quick sale. Typically this is a scene filled with pushing and shoving. There is NO structure. It is simply wild, and people act wildly trying to get everything. That is how it is for children. When there is no structure, they feel like they have been let lose in a huge "store" and everything is at their disposal whenever they want. It creates chaos. The more chaos there is, the more pushing and shoving and power struggles occur so children can try to get what they want.

Set clear limits. Make sure the children know what those limits are. Limits help promote safety and security for children. They eliminate chaos. Someone needs to take charge. If you don't take charge, the child will!!!! Children need to learn that there are rules and that these rules must be followed. They learn to respect limits.

Teach the limits—the rules, one at a time. Demonstrate for the children what it is you want them to do. For example, if a rule is "no running inside," demonstrate how to walk inside. Make it into a game walking a few steps so you "can't hear your feet." Have children take turns practicing the rule. If a child forgets and runs, simply go to the child. Get down to the child's level and calmly and quietly, remind the child to "walk quietly" in the classroom.

Establish a Connection

Children need to feel connected to someone who cares. If they are in child care, they need to have a primary caregiver that they are excited to see every day. This needs to be a person who is a safety net for times when children feel scared, lonely, or angry. This is a person who is there every day, day in and day out, week in and week out. That is one of the reasons that children act out when their primary caregiver is ill and misses work. They are missing their source of "connection." The classroom is great, but it is not the same as that person who is there for them, to greet them at the door, to smile when they have accomplished something, who listens on sad days, who really cares. That person is you. You are a difference maker in the lives of children.

Build a relationship

Katie was a petite little four year old with huge big eyes and dark curly hair when she started attending childcare. Her mom and dad had just separated. Katie never saw her daddy. One day he simply left. Her mom had just gone to work for the first time in her life. Katie's mom was depressed and constantly worrying about how to make ends meet. Little Katie wanted more and more to sit on her mom's lap and to be held and reassured. She needed this. Her mom however, was so preoccupied with her own problems that she couldn't give Katie what she needed. One day, her mom told Katie that she needed to stop trying to sit on her lap. She just didn't have time for her hugs and kisses. Those days were over. The next day Katie came to school with a tissue. She kept pressing the tissue to her cheek holding it there. Her teacher asked her what was wrong, and why she was pressing the tissue to her cheek. She said her mom wouldn't kiss her anymore. She had seen her mom blot her lipstick on the tissue and then throw the tissue in the wastebasket. Little Katie fished the tissue out and just hugged it and held it to her cheek. It held her mommy's lips on it and the kisses she didn't get anymore. Katie dragged that tissue around with her for months until it disintegrated and crumpled. Katie's mom never did kiss her or hold her again. When the tissue was gone, Katie became the class clown in childcare and then later in school. As a teenager, she used drugs and acted out. She told this story in marriage counseling with her husband. He got up and kissed her and that was the start of her feeling loved again. The moral is that children's lives are shaped by those that love them and those who refuse to love them. They all need warm and caring relationships. You never know how important your words and hugs can be and what a difference you can make in the lives of children. Imagine what would have happened to Katie if she would have had a teacher who told her she loved her and showed her how really special she was. What if she had had a teacher who let her talk and express her grief about her mom not kissing her. Imagine if she had had a teacher who reassured her and explained to her that it wasn't her fault that her mom didn't want to kiss her anymore—that her mom was probably tired and sad about something else. Imagine if she had had a teacher who said, "What can we do to help you feel better because you are so important to us?" Imagine what Katie's life would have been like if she had had a teacher who built a relationship with her. There is no one that can replace a mother's love, but there are others who can still help a child who feels unloved to feel loved. That is where you come in. You have the opportunity to build and foster caring loving relationships with each of your children.

Children's lives are shaped by those who love them and those who refuse to love them.

Three Times Twenty

A powerful way to establish a connection is to do the "three times twenty." Spend a minimum of three minutes a day for twenty consecutive days excluding week-ends, meeting with the child one-to-one. Find a private time to meet. It can be early in the morning, on the playground while someone else supervises your class, or some other special uninterrupted time. You know best your schedule and what will work for you. The important thing is to take the time to connect.

During these sacred three minutes, seek not to speak, but to get to know the heart, mind, and soul of the child. Have the child speak to you. Find out what the child likes to do on week-ends, the child's favorite hobby, the child's special friends or family members, or if they have a special inanimate friend like a stuffed animal or even a small toy car.

As you listen, simply nod your head and every now and then say, "Ah." Put your whole attention on the child. Make sure this is a time in which the other children are supervised, and you will not have any interruptions, so that your focus really can be on the child. You will get to know your child in a totally different way. The more you connect, the less you correct.

Always use the 3 A's

There are 3 important A's to remember when it comes to children that will help prevent power struggles. The first A is acceptance. Children need to be accepted for their own special unique individuality. Every child is different. Some are tall; some are short; some are thin; some are heavy; some are bright; some are slower to learn new concepts; some have ADHD; some are emotional; some don't show emotion at all. Every child is unique and different. What all children have in common is that they need to be accepted for who they are. Each child needs to be accepted for the diverse gifts the child contributes.

Acceptance does not mean accepting negative behavior. It means accepting the physical, emotional, and mental characteristics of each child.

The second A is acknowledgement. Children need to be acknowledged when they engage in appropriate behaviors. Too often, they hear what they do that is wrong, but hear very little about what they do that is right. Some children only hear their first name said in anger, "Jason, stop that!!!" They need to hear their first name said in acknowledgement. "Hi Lindsey, I'm glad that you are here today."

The third A is accomplishment. Children need opportunities to feel a sense of accomplishment. They need responsibilities that they can handle. Little jobs in the classroom help them feel like they have done something to contribute to making the classroom a better place.

Every child needs to have a special job. It can be watering a plant, cleaning up litter, dusting a shelf, setting the table, or helping you get ready for a project. It can even be to act as a special pal" to a new child or to someone who needs help. This provides a feeling of accomplishment—of helping someone else.

Chapter 3
Strategies: How to Handle Power Struggles

Mrs. Williams remembers the moments like it was yesterday. Her daughter Jenna seemed to want what she wanted almost from the moment she was born. Mrs. Williams clearly remembers Jenna, still an infant, maneuvering her small body in an un-mistakable movement of impatience designed to get her mother to nurse her NOW! One minute the baby was upright on her shoulder, and the next she was nearly horizontal. At first Mrs. Williams thought it was cute how Jenna was such a determined child, but when it became one struggle after another – Mrs. Williams felt worn out. Jenna was strong-willed from the moment she came out of the womb. That was her temperament.

Experts give credence to what many parents and teachers instinctively know -- that many children have in-born traits, such as being exceptionally strong-willed. As Jenna grows, so will the power struggles, and they may be more heated, more intense than the typical tussles between children and caretakers.

It's also important to note here that there are times that power struggles are more developmentally appropriate, and that is with two groups of children, toddlers and pre-teens. Each group is hard-wired to test the waters of independence versus the safety of staying near their caregiver's' side. It's like they are on a teeter totter one moment saying and acting, "I want it my way," and the next moment, wanting to be held and comforted like a small baby (Faull, 2000).

Understanding those factors is key to knowing what solution is likely to work in any given situation. There is no one answer to power struggles, which is why this chapter offers an assortment of strategies.

For instance, a teacher can back away from a request to have a child participate in an activity if the child is balking and the teacher feels like this is a battle best left alone. But the teacher doesn't always have that option. There's no wiggle room when it comes to situations regarding health and safety, such as when a child doesn't want to abide by rules when crossing the parking lot. Pick and choose from these options, depending on the child, and the situation, and see what works best for both of you.

Don't Fight

Instead of trying to gain the upper hand with a strong-willed child, acknowledge that is the way the child is before you respond. It's important not to see the child as an all-powerful little person who is out to make you miserable. Instead, it is important at all times to realize that this is still a child—a child who is forming patterns that will last a lifetime. The child needs your guidance to manage his or her behavior (Turecki and Tonner, 2000).

It is important to remember that there really is nothing to fight about. You are the teacher. You are the one in charge. When you become engaged in a "battle," there is always a winner and a loser. It becomes like a war with two countries battling against each other—each to win at whatever cost. The costs can become quite expensive for the countries in terms of human lives, and the costs also become very expensive in terms of human lives when there is a power struggle. While it is important for you to take charge, it is imperative that at no time, the child loses self-esteem in the process.

Instead quietly and firmly say, "I need you to _____." Describe the behavior that the child needs to do. "Samantha, I need you to sit down."

Use Power Talk Techniques

Be brief when speaking to the child. Less is truly more. The more you say, the more danger there is of the child and you getting into an argument. There is also an increased danger of the child simply tuning you out.

Be firm. Have your voice convey that you mean what you are saying. Have your entire body language show that you are expecting the child to comply. This may take practice. You may want to practice in front of a mirror. You can also record yourself. Listen to yourself on the audio or video tape. As you listen, think to yourself, "Would I listen if someone spoke like that to me?" "Was I firm, yet did I convey that I cared?" Those are important concepts you want to ensure that the children sense as you speak.

Be clear in what you say. Use simple age-appropriate words that the child understands. Sometimes, you may think the child understands, but the child saw what you were asking in a totally different way. For example, you might tell a child to put the toy away. The child puts the toy on the floor. In the child's mind, that is putting the toy away. Instead, clearly say, "I need you to put the toy on the shelf." When you clearly describe what you want done, there is a better chance that the child will comply.

Go to the child when you speak. It's important to not shout across the room. Squat down to the child's level to tell the child what it is you want.

Use pauses as you speak for emphasis. For example, say, "Jordan, (pause), I need (pause) you to put that book (pause) on the shelf."

Use a low deep voice and have your voice get deeper and lower with each word you say. The lower your voice, the more the child will listen.

Say the words, "I need" rather than "I want" or "You should" or "We need to." The words, "I need," are a much more powerful way of speaking to the child.

Co-Create Rules

Enlist children's help in creating their own rules. Interrupting a strong-willed child's playtime by saying, "It's time to clean up," in an authoritative voice, is almost certain to create a power struggle. But if the children have all helped create a chart that designates certain children do particular chores each day at a certain time of day, the teacher can refer to the chart when it's time to clean up. Then the chart, not the teacher, becomes the boss, and the power struggle may be deflected (Nelson, 1999).

Provide 2 Positive Choices

This is a very important strategy for handling strong-willed children. They want to feel like they are very important. They want to feel that their decisions matter. Frequently, because of temperament, their whole world revolves around themselves and getting what they want when they want it. It is generally not effective to say to a strong-willed child, "You do this or else!" They balk! It is also ineffective to offer a positive choice or a negative consequence. For example, it's best to avoid statements like, "Pick up the toy or you will have to clean up the whole area." Instead, it is better to offer two positive choices. "Parker, I need you to pick up the train or to pick up the blocks. Which do you prefer?" Once the child tells you, be sure and say, "Thank you."

Here are a few more examples of two positive choices. "Patricia, would you like to sit down in that chair or this one?" "Colin, would you like the green beans or the corn?" As you read this, think of situations in which you have gotten into power struggles and think of what you could have said instead.

Read Body Language and Redirect before the Struggle

Learn the telltale signs of a power struggle about to take place. Then try to head things off by distracting and redirecting children (Griffin, 2004). Example: Stevie folds his arms across his chest and shakes his head no when he's about to say no to something. Seeing this happen, the teacher distracts him with a toy or book. "Stevie, I found that book you have been wanting to read. Would you like to look at it now or do you want to look at it after circle time?"

Calm Down

In order to handle power struggles and strong-willed children, it's important that you are calm. When you lose it, the children lose it, too. Actually, when you lose your "cool," the child has just won the power struggle. The child has won because regardless if the child gets what he or she wanted, the child DID get to see you lose it! That reinforces a game that children often will continue playing called, "Get the teacher."

Use deep breathing to calm down. Sit down in a comfortable chair or stand up straight wherever you are. Have your feet firmly planted on the floor. Now imagine that your stomach has a balloon in it. Every time you inhale, the balloon expands, and every time you exhale, the balloon deflates. Watch your stomach as you do this. As you inhale and exhale, breathe in peace, calm and strength, then let go of anger, frustration, and confusion. Spend as much time as you can cooling down. You are setting a great example for your children, and you're doing the right thing by not engaging in an argument when you are upset.

Walk the Magical Circle

Put colored tape on the floor in a large circle shape. When children are upset and need to calm down, direct them to walk the circle, heel to toe, until they feel calm. When they feel they can make wise choices and feel calm, they stop walking.

Laugh Together

Sometimes being silly is just the trick for breaking through a power struggle in the making. This is not about laughing at any child, but simply about bursting forth with joy. It definitely gets the attention of children when the class is joyful. If a child's face has become tense and serious, one fun game to play is "Find the Smile." Have all children start looking around the room to find smiles. They look in their shoes, out the window, under a table, until they are all smiling and laughing.

Use Novelty

Children love novelty. Do something unexpected to change the entire mood of the classroom before any power struggles develop. Have children all stand up and sing a song or dance a dance. The more fun you are having, the less power struggles you will have.

Have a Wise Choice Chair

This is a voluntary place that both you and the children go when you are feeling you need to make a wise choice about something to prevent classroom problems. It is a nice comfy chair. It might even be a rocking chair. It could also be a couple of cozy pillows on the floor. Sometimes, there is just so much going on in the early childhood classroom that it can get difficult to think straight. When the child goes to the Wise Choice Chair, the child thinks about all of the options available and then strives to choose one that will make the classroom a better place. Give examples. Demonstrate doing this. Go to the chair, sit down, and tell them about choices you have. Then make a wise choice. Next, invite other children to sit in the chair when they need to make wise choices. You are teaching children to pause and reflect before they engage in behavior.

The Paper Bag Trick

When there is a power struggle, instead of arguing with the child, ask the child to tell you all the things that he or she can do that are appropriate in the classroom. Write each choice down on a piece of paper. Put them all into a bag. The child lifts one out of the bag and that is the child's choice for that situation.

Share Stories and Books

There any many excellent books and stories about how to deal with anger, as well as books which explain why it's important to cooperate. Choose some of these to share and discuss with the children. Discuss positive appropriate behaviors for the classroom.

WHEN YOU'RE MAD AND YOU KNOW IT, E. Crary and S. Steelsmith. Parenting Press, 1996.

WHERE IS LEOPARD: A TALE OF COOPERATION, W. Wax and M. Terry. Reader's Digest, 2006.

THE GROUCHY LADYBUG, E. Carle. Harper and Row, 1977.

Whisper into Child's Ear

When a child is really upset and argumentative, calmly whisper into the child's ear. First, it is distracting to the child that is on a tirade to have you squat down next to the child and whisper. Secondly, the quieter your own voice, the quieter the child becomes. Thirdly, it is very calming for the child when you are calm and whispering. The child gets quieter and quieter as the child listens intently to what you are saying.

Re-Channel Their Leadership Abilities

The strong-willed child is generally a strong leader. They have great leadership abilities. They know how to persevere. This is shown when they hold out and hold out to get their way.

They know how to "read" people. They intuitively seem to sense where people are more sensitive and vulnerable. They often choose just the right time and place to make their arguments—these are times where the adult will not be as strong.

They know how to manage others. Because they are so strong, others generally heed them. The other children in the classroom, for whatever the reason, often do what these children want them to do.

Take advantage of this and harness the leadership ability that strong-willed children have. Redirect them to doing projects that help others. Involve them in creating ideas. You are actually training them to use the gifts they have in a much more appropriate way.

Get Creative

Take a totally unexpected approach to shake things up. For the child who has been refusing to come to the lunch table, enlist the child's help in following a line of imaginary caterpillars to the table. If the child likes trucks, make a make-believe highway filled with trucks (Pantley, 1996).

Make Fewer Requests

It has been found that children may be on the receiving end of up to 40 requests from adults in an hour. This is an overwhelming amount for anyone. After awhile, children tune adults out. Reduce the amount of requests to the really important ones. Acknowledge the children when they are cooperative.

Use Gestures and Props to Show What You Want

Some children are visual or tactile learners. They really don't understand what you mean when you give auditory instructions. You can gently place a hand on a child's back to help guide the child somewhere. You can show the children a picture of what they are supposed to do. All of these are cues to help children understand what you want. It stops a battle before it begins.

Speak "Childese"

When you run up against resistance from a child—especially a young child, it is helpful to simply repeat back what the child says (Karp,2004).

When Sally says "No, no, no!" her caretaker repeats her words back to her, "No, no, no! You don't want to go inside!" Pause for emphasis, because you've got her attention now. Repeat "No, no, no! You don't want to go inside! I understand. It really was fun. It is time to go inside now for lunch."

Use "Regardless" and "Nevertheless."

When a child starts to battle with you, simply listen to what the child says. Then calmly and firmly say, "Sounds like you want to…, nevertheless, I need you to _____." Here's an example. Carina is pushing and pushing to stay outside when it's time to come in. Very calmly say, "Sounds like you are upset. Nevertheless, I need you to come inside now." You can substitute the word "regardless" for the word "nevertheless."

Teach Children to Say OKEY DOKEY.

Have a class game. You make a request and children respond, "okey dokey." Here's an example. "It's time to clean up and get ready for lunch." Entire class responds, "Okey dokey!" They love it. It feels more like a game than an order.

Chapter 4
Precautions with Sensitive Children

The truth is that you have to take precautions with all children any time you speak. The words you say can be damaging to all children. Therefore, it is important to choose your words carefully before speaking.

Whether by temperament, or by training, some children are more sensitive than others, in addition, even the most easy-going child may be overly sensitive from time to time. This doesn't mean you have to tiptoe around feelings in order to avoid power struggles, but you may have use special techniques to prevent things from escalating.

Use "I Feel" Statements

The word "you" can sound accusing to a sensitive child. Instead, state how you feel. Tell what you see, and then explain what you want. Example: "I feel scared that one of us will become lost when we don't hold hands in this big crowd. I need for us to hold hands."

The Word "Bad"

It's important to never ever say the word "bad" to a child. This includes telling the child that his or her behavior is bad. To tell a child that a behavior is bad is the same as telling the child that the child is bad. For example, Ms. Carson was asked to mentor a brand new teacher. Ms. Carson watched the teacher teach, and then they met to discuss the observation. What if Ms. Carson said to the new teacher, "You have a great smile and enthusiasm; however, your teaching is bad." How would the new teacher feel? That is the same way a child would feel. Instead of making a judgment statement about the child's misbehavior, simply tell the child to "Stop!" Then tell the child the new and more appropriate behavior that the child needs to do.

> *"Jason, stop! I need you to come inside the building now."*

Be Understanding, but Persistent

The child who resists you by telling you that he or she wants to stay outside for five more minutes or draw one more picture needs you to be understanding, but persistent. "Karen, I know that you want to stay outside, you will get to go outside later. I need you to go to go inside now." Or, "I know that you want to color one more picture, but I need you to clean up the art supplies now."

Chapter 5
More Important Communication Skills

Any and all of the techniques learned will be most effective if you remember to add these other aspects of successful communication:

Eye Contact.

For most children, it's good to make eye contact. Squat down to the child's level, look at the child, and then speak. Avoid staring, which can be intimidating. Look directly at the child with a firm and steady gaze.

There are some children who have a real problem with eye contact. It can be a cultural issue. It can also be a sensitivity issue. Squat down to speak to these children. However, instead of looking directly into the eyes, look above the eyes at the forehead. That way you are still making contact, but it is less intimidating for the children.

Choose the Setting Wisely

Be cautious about where you approach the child. Some children are easily embarrassed. You may have to take the child aside to speak so that the child is not embarrassed in front of peers.

Say What You Need and then Turn Your Attention to Others

All children appreciate the opportunity to save face with their peers. For example, state calmly and clearly that Zoe needs to wear a smock while painting or she can do another non-painting activity. Ask her which one she chooses. If it is taking a long time for a response, stay tuned to her, but turn your attention to another child. Turn to her friend Austin, and offer to help him with his painting smock. This gives her a positive example to follow while deflecting an all-eyes-on-Zoe confrontation.

Provide Transition Cues

If the same power struggle keeps surfacing again and again, give the child a cue before stating your need. This gives the child time to absorb what is about to happen. This helps prevent the child's knee-jerk reaction to something the child really doesn't want to do.

Here's an example. Jason doesn't like to stop playing to come inside for lunch. By telling Jason, "Five minutes until we stop to go in for lunch," he has time to absorb what is for him, bad news. He is better prepared when you do say, "It's time to come inside now and have lunch."

You can also use a timer with this approach, therefore adding a visual cue to this effective way to avoid power struggles

with children who have a hard time with transitions in general (Loomis, 2002).

Know When to Let the Child Win

There is a time in every child's life when they need the "wise gift" of an adult who steps back instead of insisting that their needs get met. You will know this moment, and it will not feel like "giving in," or "stuffing your feelings," but an opportunity to build a bond with the child. It's really not about you losing, but about you gaining as you and the child connect. This is not the same as giving in. It's about choosing the appropriate times for confronting a child and the times to simply let it go!

References

Appelbaum, M. (2007). No More Tantrums. Houston, TX: Appelbaum Publishing

Appelbaum, M. (2000). How to Talk to Kids so They Listen. Houston, TX: Appelbaum Publishing.

Faull, J. (2002). Unplugging Power Struggles With Your Kids. Seattle, WA: Parenting Press.

Griffin, L. (2004). The Promise of Proactive Parenting. San Diego, CA: Avantine Press.

Karp, H. (2004) The Happiest Toddler on the Block: The New Way to Stop the Daily Battle of Wills and Raise a Secure and Well-Behaved One- to Four-Year-Old. New York, NY: Bantam Books.

Loomis, T. (2000). Tempering an Iron-Willed Child, New York, NY: Wondertime.

Nelson, J. (1999). Over 50 Ways to Avoid Power Struggles in the Home and the Classroom. Orem, UT: Positive Discipline.

Pantley, E. (1996) Kid Cooperation: How to Stop Yelling, Nagging and Pleading and Get Kids to Cooperate. Oakland, CA: Pantley Publication.

Turecki & Tonner. (2000). The Difficult Child. New York, NY: Bantam Press.

Appendix

The following pages have a self-instructional examination you may be able to use to get Continuing Education Units in your state. Please check with your state's licensing department regarding self-study courses before submitting your test for grading. Not all states recognize self-study as a way to fulfill clock hour and continuing education requirements.

States that recognize self-study as of August 2008

AL   AR   AZ   CO   CT   FL   IA   IN   KS   ME   MN   MS
NE   NJ   NV   OK   OR   PA   TN   TX   VA   WI

Those fulfilling their CDA requirements may use this course.

To receive Continuing Education Units and Clock Hours is easy. Make as many copies as needed of the Examination at the back of this book for each individual needing a Certificate. Send one copy per person and $9.00 per person.

You will receive a Certificate of Completion for Clock Hours and Continuing Education Units and your graded examination back for each person for which you have enclosed $9.00.

To pass the examination, you must score 75% or better. There is a $5.00 retake per person if needed. However, if you have read the course materials and answered all of the questions, you will do well. We look forward to awarding you with your beautiful Certificate of Completion.

You can earn more clock hours using other self-instructional materials by writing to the address below, calling 1 800-23-CHILD, or checking www.atiseminars.org.

ATI/Clock Hours and CEU's
104 Industrial Boulevard, Suite A
Sugar Land, Texas 77478

Registration Form for NO MORE BATTLES
Clock Hours and Continuing Education Units

Number of copies of examinations _____ **(Note: There must be one per person.)**
Names of individuals completing examinations (NOTE: Put each individual's name on each examination.)
Please Print

_____   _____
_____   _____
_____   _____
_____   _____

Name of Individual or Center to mail Certificate(s)_____
Street_____
City_____State_____Zip_____
Number of copies of examination_____ (There must be one per person.)
Amount of money enclosed $_____ (There must be $9.00 per person.)
Pay by check of Master Card_____ Visa_____ Discover_____ American Express_____
Card Number_____Expiration Date_____
Signature_____
MAKE YOUR CHECK PAYABLE TO ATI AND MAIL WITH THIS FORM TO:
ATI/Clock Hours and CEU's
104 Industrial, Suite A Sugar Land, Texas 77478
For further information, or to order books, call 1 800-23-CHILD.

No More Battles * Maryln Appelbaum
69

NO MORE BATTLES

Name_____

Street_____

City_____ State_____ Zip_____

Work Phone (____)_____ Home Phone (____)_____

Directions: Answer the fill-in questions on the following pages. These questions are designed to help you review what you have learned. You will not be graded on these questions as each child is unique and so is each teacher. However, we will be looking at your answers to make sure you have **filled them in.** You will be **graded on the 25 multiple choice and true and false questions** that begin on page 77. Best wishes to you.

Describe your most difficult problem with power struggles.

Describe what you have done in the past to handle this problem.

Implement 5 strategies you have learned in this book, the date implemented, and the result. Have fun.

STRATEGY	DATE IMPLEMENTED	RESULT

Directions: Choose the best answer to each of the following questions.

_____1. A reason children become strong-willed is:
      a.   They are born that way.
      b.   They are trained to be that way.
      c.   Too much sugar in their diet.
      d.   A and B.

_____2. The parents of strong-willed children:
      a.   Don't love them enough to say "no."
      b.   Often give in.
      c.   Never give in.
      d.   Aren't likely to be frustrated.

_____3. A strategy that prevents battles with strong-willed children is:
      a.   Walk on eggshells so you don't provoke them.
      b.   Get angry.
      c.   Loosen up on your rules.
      d.   None of the above.

_____4. When children have no limits:
     a. They feel insecure.
     b. Their world can feel chaotic.
     c. Power struggles often happen.
     d. All of the above.

_____5. "Three times 20" refers to:
     a. Holding a stuffed turtle.
     b. Sixty opportunities for resolving power struggles.
     c. Spending three minutes a day for 20 consecutive days with the child one-on-one.
     d. None of the above.

Directions: Circle T for True or F for False in each of the following statements.

True   False

T   F   6. It's okay to tell a child that behavior is bad.

T   F   7. Acceptance, acknowledgement and accomplishment are the three A's.

T   F   8. Giving children 2 positive choices is a strategy for power struggles.

T   F   9. Children who are strong-willed can grow into powerful leaders.

T   F   10. Laughing together rarely works in a power struggle situation.

T   F   11. The magical circle works by giving children a place to calm themselves.

T   F   12. Children need to be forced to go to the Wise Choice Chair.

T   F   13. It is not important for the adult to be calm during a "battle."

T   F   14. Children may hear up to 40 requests an hour from adults.

T   F   15. It's important for the adult to make all rules alone to take charge.

T   F   16. Novelty is an effective tool for preventing power struggles.

T   F   17. There is no need to acknowledge children engaging in appropriate behavior.

T   F   18. The paper bag trick is a bag filled with candy for wise choices.

T   F   19. Teach children as a class to say "regardless" to requests.

T　F　20. Teach children as a class to say, "OKEY DOKEY" to requests.

T　F　21. Use as many words as possible when resolving a power struggle.

T　F　22. Give a child a five-minute warning to try and pre-empt problem transitions from one activity to another.

T　F　23. The word "you" can sound accusatory to a sensitive child.

T　F　24. Teach children to speak "childese" to get what they need.

T　F　25. The setting for confronting children is not as important. It's your words.